MAY 2 8 2009

WEAPONS OF WAR

WEAPONS OF THE

AMERICAN INDIANS

by Matt Doeden

Reading Consultant:
Barbara J. Fox
Reading Specialist
North Carolina State University

Content Consultant:
Melodie Andrews
Associate Professor of Early American History
Minnesota State University, Mankato

Capstone
press

Mankato, Minnesota

Blazers is published by Capstone Press,
151 Good Counsel Drive, P.O. Box 669, Mankato, Minnesota 56002.
www.capstonepress.com

Library of Congress Cataloging-in-Publication Data
Doeden, Matt.
    Weapons of the American Indians / by Matt Doeden.
    p. cm. — (Blazers. Weapons of war)
    Includes bibliographical references and index.
    Summary: "Describes American Indian weapons, including hand-to-hand
combat and long range weapons" — Provided by publisher.
    ISBN-13: 978-1-4296-2334-6 (hardcover)
    ISBN-10: 1-4296-2334-9 (hardcover)
1. Indians of North America — Warfare — Juvenile literature. 2. Indian
weapons — North America — Juvenile literature. I. Title. II. Series.
E98.W2D64 2009
970.04'97 — dc22   2008030821

Editorial Credits
Mandy Robbins, editor; Alison Thiele, set designer; Kyle Grenz, book designer;
    Jo Miller, photo researcher

Photo Credits
Alamy/North Wind Picture Archives, 5
Art Resource, N.Y./Werner Forman, 20–21 (slingshot), 25 (slingshot),
    29 (armor)
Corbis/Bettmann, 6, 28; Brian A. Vikander, 26–27; Carl & Ann Purcell,
    20–21 (atlatl), 25 (atlatl); Christie's Images, 9 (tomahawk),
    13 (war club with blade); Werner Forman, 13 (blunt war club),
    26 (shield), 29 (shield)
Getty Images Inc./Hulton Archive/MPI, 9 (American Indian), 16
The Image Works/Topham/Werner Forman, 11, 13 (obsidian blade)
iStockphoto/Hulton Archive, 12; Joseph Jean Rolland Dube,
    cover (tomahawk), 13 (tomahawk); KD Taggart, 18–19 (arrows),
    24 (arrows)
Nativestock.com/Marilyn Angel Wynn, 24 (bow), 25 (blowgun), 25 (rifle)
Newscom/Getty Images/Hulton Archive, 22–23
Shutterstock/Carolina K. Smith M.D. 19 (arrowhead top center);
    Debra James, cover (armor); Kenneth V. Pilon, cover (arrowhead),
    18–19 (arrowheads), 18 (arrowhead left), 24 (arrowheads);
    Snowleopard1, 10, 13 (stone blade); Wellford Tiller,
    19 (arrowhead center)
SuperStock, Inc., 15, 29 (wall)

TABLE OF CONTENTS

WEAPONS WITH MANY USES

An American Indian hunter waits in a quiet forest. A deer wanders nearby. The hunter shoots his bow and arrow. Ping! His people will eat well tonight.

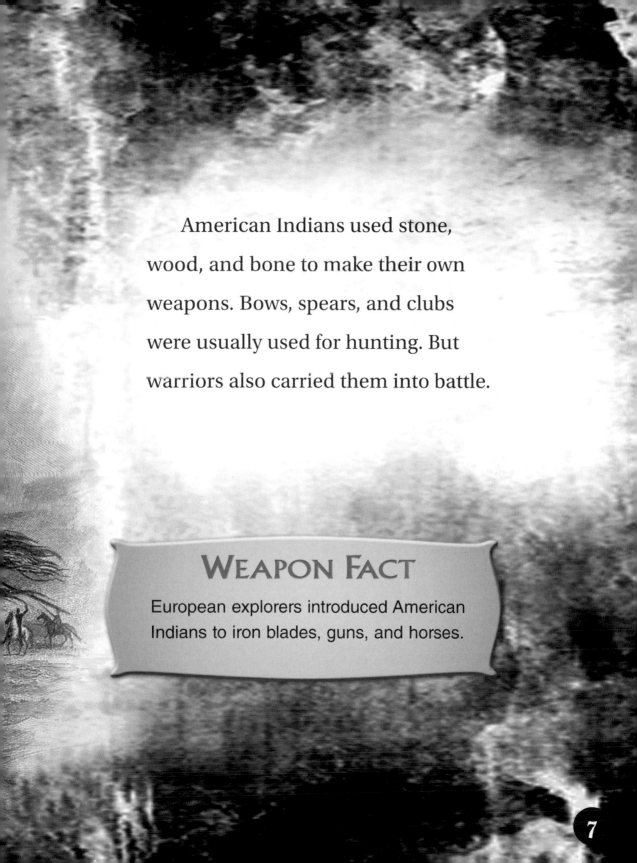

American Indians used stone, wood, and bone to make their own weapons. Bows, spears, and clubs were usually used for hunting. But warriors also carried them into battle.

WEAPON FACT

European explorers introduced American Indians to iron blades, guns, and horses.

CHOPPING, STABBING, AND BASHING

American Indians used hatchets to hunt and to chop wood. Warriors also threw them at enemies in battle. The **tomahawk** is the most famous hatchet.

tomahawk – a small ax once used by some American Indians as a weapon or tool

tomahawk with
metal blade

9

stone blades

Warriors used the sharp edges of
stone blades to slash and stab enemies.
The Hupa Indians carried **obsidian** blades.

obsidian – a dark glass formed by cooling
volcanic lava

WEAPON FACT

A Beaver-Tail knife had a wide double-edged blade. It looked like a canoe paddle.

obsidian blade

war club

American Indians made war clubs out of stone or wood. Sometimes blades were attached to the clubs. Warriors bashed enemies with clubs during battle. Hunters also attacked animals with clubs.

HANDHELD WEAPONS

obsidian blade

stone blade

war club with metal blade

tomahawk with stone blade

war club with blunt end

Spears, Bows, and Slingshots

The spear is the oldest American Indian weapon. Spears had long wooden **shafts** and stone **heads**. Hunters threw spears at animals. Warriors flung them at enemies.

shaft – the long, narrow rod of a spear or arrow

head — the top end of a spear or arrow where the blade is

bow and arrow

Bows fired arrows farther than a spear could be thrown. Most American Indian arrows had wooden shafts. The most common bow was made from one piece of wood. It was called a "self-bow."

WEAPON FACT

Arctic Indians often used bone instead of wood for arrow shafts.

arrows

Arrowheads were made of stone. Feathers added to the arrow shafts helped the arrows fly straight.

arrowheads

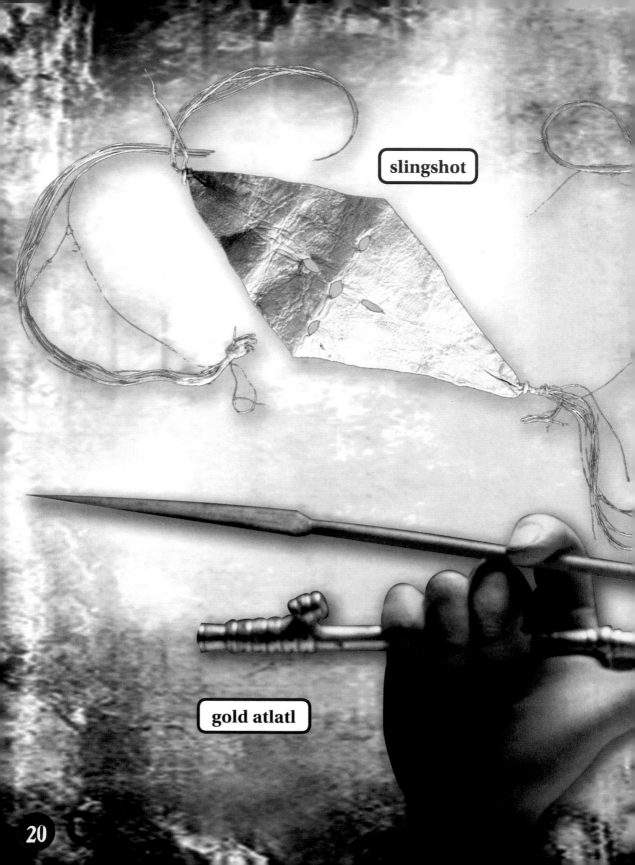

slingshot

gold atlatl

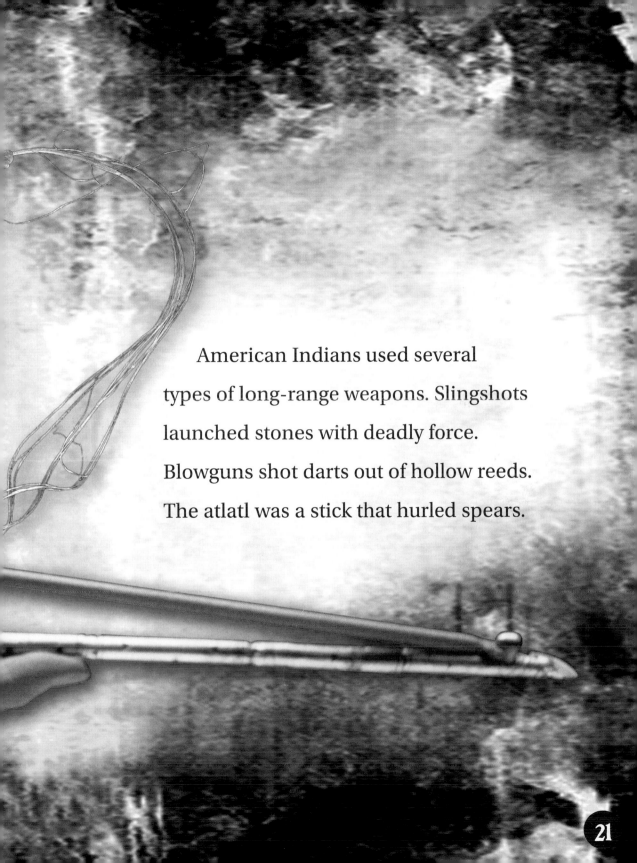

American Indians used several types of long-range weapons. Slingshots launched stones with deadly force. Blowguns shot darts out of hollow reeds. The atlatl was a stick that hurled spears.

In the late 1400s, Europeans brought guns to North America. The first guns often missed their targets. They were also slow to load. As guns improved, many American Indians used them.

WEAPON FACT

American Indians also used European swords. These metal swords were sharper than stone blades.

LONG-RANGE WEAPONS

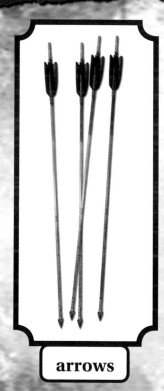

arrows

arrowheads

self-bow

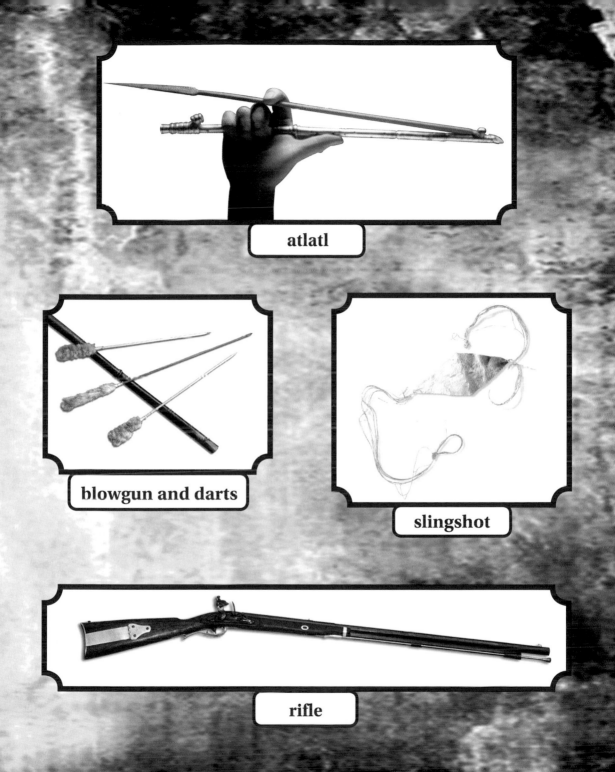

atlatl

blowgun and darts

slingshot

rifle

WEAK DEFENSES

Some American Indians carried shields. Shields were round and made of wood or animal skin. Warriors decorated them with meaningful symbols.

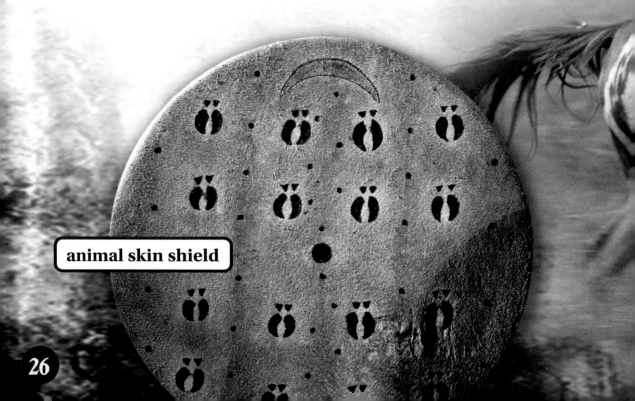

animal skin shield

American Indians wore **armor** made of
wood or bone. But it didn't protect them from
the Europeans. Over time, Europeans took
over the American Indians' land and changed
their way of life forever.

armor — a protective covering worn by
warriors during battle

DEFENSES

village wall

bone armor

animal skin shield

GLOSSARY

armor (AR-muhr) — a protective covering worn by warriors during battle

atlatl (AHT-laht-l) — a throwing stick used to launch a spear

hatchet (HACH-it) — a small ax used mainly as a tool but also as a weapon

head (HED) — the top end of a spear where the blade is located

obsidian (ob-SI-dee-en) — a dark glass formed by cooling volcanic lava

shaft (SHAFT) — the long narrow rod of an arrow or spear

tomahawk (TOM-uh-hawk) — a small ax once used by American Indians as a tool and a weapon

READ MORE

Doeden, Matt. *Weapons of Ancient Times.* Weapons of War. Mankato, Minn.: Capstone Press, 2009.

Helbrough, Emma. *A Day in the Life of a Native American.* A Day in the Life. New York: PowerKids Press, 2008.

Herbst, Judith. *The History of Weapons.* Major Inventions Through History. Minneapolis: Twenty-First Century Books, 2006.

INTERNET SITES

FactHound offers a safe, fun way to find educator-approved Internet sites related to this book.

Here's what you do:

1. Visit www.*facthound.com*
2. Choose your grade level.
3. Begin your search.

This book's ID number is 9781429623346.

FactHound will fetch the best sites for you!

INDEX